KENTUCKY MOUNTAIN SQUARE DANCING

(RUNNING SET)

Copyright EFDSS 1982
THE ENGLISH FOLK DANCE AND SONG SOCIETY
Cecil Sharp House, 2 Regent's Park Road, London, NW1 7AY.

PAT NAPIER'S OBSERVATIONS

Each community throughout the mountains where square dancing was done used to have figures that they would dance. Perhaps when one of the dancers moved from this community to another, he would teach his version of the figure and it would change a little in transit: then, too, people used their imagination to make up new figures.

Traditionally, the square dance was done in a 'set' of four couples; with time this changed into the 'Big Set' where any number (divisible by four) may enter the set. The formation is one large circle with first couples on the inside facing out to second couples.

Most of the square dancing moved from the home to the 'road houses', 'honky tonks' or 'jennybarns', as they were called.

GENERAL INSTRUCTIONS

The Music:

The dance is smooth and exciting to do to such tunes as: Cripple Creek, Old Joe Clark, Flop-Eared Mule, Pretty Little Widder, Sugar in my Coffee-O, Sugar in the Gourd, etc, etc.

The Step:

The step will vary with the dancers; some prefer a fast walk, some a slow running step, some use very few foot movements and change-steps, while others use a great variety. The fancy foot work was usually left to the more advanced dancers.

The Caller:

It is up to the Caller to keep the dance moving along. It depends upon the size of the room and the number of 'sets' being run, as to whether or not the Caller will call from the floor while dancing or use the public address system.

Points for Calling — Know your Calls

   Give them clearly and distinctly and in time for the dancers to know what is coming next.

<u>Points for Calling</u> — Call the name of the figure before giving the call-lines.

When dancing with a new group, find out what figures it knows.

Practise your Calling in private.

*****

The tunes suggested on page 2 are printed in American Square Dance Tunes - obtainable from The Folk Shop, Cecil Sharp House, 2 Regent's Park Road, London, NW1 7AY. Tel: 01 485 2206

The following figures are in addition to those printed in The Country Dance Book by Cecil J. Sharp, part 5, published by Novello & Company Ltd., but now out of print.

DO-SI-DO

There are two forms of the do-si-do which are generally used, one is described in Country Dance: Book 5, page 25, the other is described here:

DO AND A DO AND A LITTLE MORE DO

CHICKEN IN THE BREADPAN SCRATCHING UP DOUGH

ONE MORE CHANGE AND HOME YOU GO

After a figure is danced by two couples the call do-si-do is given by the Caller. The two couples face. The gent's partner is on his right with her left hand in his right hand. The gent allows the lady to pass in front of him, around behind him and back to her place (both couples do this at the same time). The partners hold hands through part of this figure and drop hands when the lady is passing behind the gent. The gent then swings his corner (opposite) lady with a two-hand swing once around then swings his own partner once around. The leading couple go on to the next couple while the other couple (the 'second' or 'number two' or 'even') fall back into their original place in the set.

AROUND THE WORLD

CHASE THE RABBIT, CHASE THE SQUIRREL
CHASE THAT PRETTY GIRL AROUND THE WORLD
EVERYBODY SWING
CHASE THE RABBIT, CHASE THE FOX
CHASE THAT HOBO OUT OF HIS SOCKS
EVERYBODY SWING

<u>CHASE THE RABBIT, CHASE THE SQUIRREL</u>
<u>CHASE THAT PRETTY GIRL AROUND THE WORLD</u>

The first lady lead round to the right of the set, behind couples number two, three and four. She is followed by the first gent. The call-line is distributed throughout the movement. When the first lady returns to her home position she turns to face the first gent.

<u>EVERYBODY SWING</u>

Partners turn each other once round clockwise with the two-hand swing.

<u>CHASE THE RABBIT, CHASE THE FOX</u>
<u>CHASE THAT HOBO OUT OF HIS SOCKS</u>

As in the first call-line, except that the first gent leads round the set and is followed by the first lady.

<u>EVERYBODY SWING</u>

Partners swing.

*****

Optional call:

CHASE THE RABBIT, CHASE THE COON
CHASE THAT PRETTY GIRL AROUND THE MOON
FIRST COUPLE SWING
CHASE THE RABBIT, CHASE THE FOX
CHASE THAT HOBO OUT OF HIS SOCKS
EVERYBODY SWING

ELBOW SWING

TWO GENTS SWING WITH AN ELBOW SWING
NOW YOUR OPPOSITE WITH AN ELBOW SWING
NOW THE TWO GENTS WITH THE SALE OLE THING
NOW YOUR PARTNERS WITH A TURKEY WING
CIRCLE FOUR

<u>TWO GENTS SWING WITH AN ELBOW SWING</u>

The first and second gents link right elbows and swing once-and-a-half round.

<u>NOW YOUR OPPOSITE WITH AN ELBOW SWING</u>

The first gent and the second lady link left elbows and swing once round, while the first lady and the second gent link left elbows and swing once round.

<u>NOW THE TWO GENTS WITH THE SAME OLE THING</u>

(Same as first call-line)

<u>NOW YOUR PARTNERS WITH A TURKEY WING</u>

Partners link left elbows and swing once round, the man leaving his partner on his right.

<u>CIRCLE FOUR</u>

FOUR - LEAF CLOVER

ODD COUPLE MAKE A FOUR - LEAF CLOVER
BREAK IT EVEN

ODD COUPLE MAKE A FOUR - LEAF CLOVER

(The two couples circle to the left and, if directed, back to the right.)

The second couple make an arch. The first couple, still holding hands with the second couple, pass under the arch. The first gent turns counter-clockwise, while the first lady turns clockwise (all still holding hands).

This makes the four - leaf clover.

BREAK IT EVEN

The odd (first) couple make an arch for the even (second) couple to pass through. The second gent and second lady turn away from each other and all are back in a circle of four.

(The whole figure is done without breaking the ring.)

*****

This figure may be doubled by having the even couple make the four - leaf clover and letting the odd couple break it.

LADY 'ROUND THE LADY

LADY 'ROUND THE LADY, GENT ALSO
LADY 'ROUND THE GENT, GENT DON'T GO
COUPLE FOUR

LADY 'ROUND THE LADY, GENT ALSO

The first lady, followed by the first gent, leads between the second couple, and to the left round the second lady.

LADY 'ROUND THE GENT, GENT DON'T GO

The first lady, this time alone, leads between the second couple, and goes to the right round the second gent. The first gent dances in place.

COUPLE FOUR

*****

This figure is sometimes called as follows:

LADY 'ROUND THE LADY, GENT SOLO
LADY 'ROUND THE GENT, GENT DON'T GO

The first lady leads between the second couple, and to the left round the second lady, while the first gent dances in place.

Then the first lady leads between the second couple, and to the right round the second gent, while the first gent dances in place, as in the second part of the figure above. (If the figure is danced in this way, the first gent doesn't do much dancing. All the first lady does is a figure of eight round the second couple.)

MOUNTAINEER LOOP

or

Cowboy or Buffalo Loop

CIRCLE FOUR -- FIRST COUPLE - MOUNTAINEER LOOP
CIRCLE LEFT -- SECOND COUPLE - MOUNTAINEER LOOP
CIRCLE LEFT

CIRCLE FOUR
FIRST COUPLE - MOUNTAINEER LOOP

The two couples take hands four and circle left once round. The second couple raise their inside hands to make an arch. The first couple go under the arch, drop hands (only the first couple drop hands), the first gent goes to his left round the second lady, while the first lady goes to her right round the second gent. The second gent turns clockwise under his right arm, while the second lady turns counter-clockwise under her left arm.

CIRCLE LEFT

The first and second couples take hands four and circle once round to the left.

SECOND COUPLE - MOUNTAINEER LOOP

The action above is reversed. The first couple make an arch for the second couple to go under. The second couple go under the arch, drop hands, the second gent goes to the left round the first lady, while the second lady goes to the right round the first gent. The first gent turns clockwise under his right arm, while the first lady turns counter-clockwise under her left arm.

CIRCLE LEFT or CIRCLE FOUR or COUPLE FOUR

OCEAN WAVE

or

GARDEN GATE

OCEAY UP (Pronounced "Oh She")
OCEAY BACK
OCEAY AROUND THAT OUTSIDE TRACK
CIRCLE FOUR

OCEAN WAVE
OCEAY UP

The first couple take hands in the promenade position (right in right over left in left) and move four steps forward between the second couple. The second couple move forward four steps on the outside of the first couple.

OCEAY BACK

The first couple turn in place, still holding hands, and move four steps forward between the second couple to their original places. The second lady and second gent turn and move back to their original places.

OCEAY AROUND THAT OUTSIDE TRACK

This call-line is the same as OCEAY UP and OCEAY BACK, and means that the second couple will take hands in the promenade position and move between the first couple, turn and come back to place, while the first gent and first lady go on the outside "track". (The two couples reverse action.)

CIRCLE FOUR

This figure is sometimes called "Butterfly".

OLD ARKANSAS

or

SWING YOUR PA

SWING YOUR PA
SWING YOUR MA
DON'T FORGET OLD ARKANSAS
COUPLE FOUR

SWING YOUR PA

The first couple face the second couple. The first lady turn the second gent with both hands once round clockwise.

SWING YOUR MA

The first lady turn the second lady with both hands once round clockwise.

DON'T FORGET OLD ARKANSAS

The first lady turn the first gent (her partner) with both hands once round clockwise and stay to the right of him.

COUPLE FOUR

OLD SIDE DOOR

or

LITTLE SIDE DOOR

AROUND THIS COUPLE, LADY IN THE LEAD
GENT FALLS THROUGH AND HE TAKES THE LEAD
LADY FALLS THROUGH THE OLD SIDE DOOR
SIDE COUPLE SWING
AND COUPLE FOUR

OLD SIDE DOOR
AROUND THIS COUPLE, LADY IN THE LEAD

The second couple drop hands and stand facing the inside of the ring, while the first lady, followed by the first gent, moves to the right of the second couple and goes behind the second couple.

GENT FALLS THROUGH AND HE TAKES THE LEAD

The first gent passes between the second couple from behind, while the first lady goes on round the second couple. The first gent is now in the lead. He moves to the right, behind the second couple, while the first lady follows behind him.

LADY FALLS THROUGH THE OLD (LITTLE) SIDE DOOR
SIDE COUPLE SWING

The first lady passes between the second couple from behind and is swung by the first gent who has gone on round the second couple. The second couple swing once round in place.

AND COUPLE FOUR

The first and second couples join hands in a ring and circle to the left.

RIGHT HANDS 'CROSS

RIGHT HANDS 'CROSS (AND HOW ARE YOU)
LEFT HANDS BACK (I'M FINE, THANK YOU)
LADIES CHANGE
GENTS THE SAME
CIRCLE FOUR

RIGHT HANDS 'CROSS (AND HOW ARE YOU)

The first and second couples take right hands across.

LEFT HANDS BACK (I'M FINE, THANK YOU)

Take left hands across.

LADIES CHANGE

The two gents drop left hands. The two ladies, still holding left hands, exchange places and then drop hands. The ladies pass left shoulder.

GENTS THE SAME

Without taking hands, the two gents exchange places, passing by the right shoulder.

CIRCLE FOUR

Note: The call-line "LADIES CHANGE" is sometimes confused with "LADIES CHAIN". If there is confusion, call "LADIES CROSS OVER" and "GENTS CROSS OVER".

The call "FALL BACK GENTS, WHILE THE GIRLS KEEP TURNING" is a nice change for this figure.

SWING AT THE WALL

AROUND THIS COUPLE AND SWING AT THE WALL
BACK TO THE CENTRE AND SWING IN THE HALL
CIRCLE FOUR

AROUND THIS COUPLE AND SWING AT THE WALL

The first gent go to the left round the second lady, while the first lady go to the right round the second gent. The first couple swing once round behind the second couple - ("Swing at the wall").

BACK TO THE CENTRE AND SWING IN THE HALL

The first gent go to the right round the second lady (on the same side as he went before), while the first lady go back to the left round the second gent. Here the first couple swing again. (For variation, the second couple can sometimes sneak in a swing.)

CIRCLE FOUR

SWING WHEN YOU MEET

AROUND THIS COUPLE, SWING WHEN YOU MEET
BACK TO THE CENTRE AND SWING YOUR SWEET
AROUND THIS COUPLE, SWING ONCE MORE
BACK TO THE CENTRE AND SWING ALL FOUR
CIRCLE FOUR

AROUND THIS COUPLE, SWING WHEN YOU MEET

The second couple stand in place while the first couple, (the first gent moving to his left, the first lady to the right), move round behind the second couple and swing once round.

BACK TO THE CENTRE AND SWING YOUR SWEET

The first couple move round in front of the second couple back to their place (going back on the same side as they went) and swing once round. (The second couple do not swing.)

AROUND THIS COUPLE, SWING ONCE MORE

(Same as first call-line)

BACK TO THE CENTRE AND SWING ALL FOUR

The first couple move round in front of the second couple back to their place and swing once round; while the second couple swing once round - two-hand swing once round.

CIRCLE FOUR

Note: This figure is practically the same as "TAKE A LITTLE PEEK", except that a swing is added behind the second couple.

See page 15

TAKE A LITTLE PEEK (PEEP)

```
AROUND THIS COUPLE, TAKE A LITTLE PEEK
BACK TO THE CENTRE AND SWING YOUR SWEET
AROUND THIS COUPLE, PEEK ONCE MORE
BACK TO THE CENTRE AND SWING ALL FOUR
COUPLE FOUR
```

AROUND THIS COUPLE, TAKE A LITTLE PEEK

The second couple stand still, while the first couple, (first gent moving to the left, first lady to the right), advance forward to where they can see each other behind the second couple.

BACK TO THE CENTRE AND SWING YOUR SWEET

The first couple move back to their place and swing once round. Second couple do not swing.

AROUND THIS COUPLE, PEEK ONCE MORE

(As in the first call-line)

BACK TO THE CENTRE AND SWING ALL FOUR

First couple move back to their place and both couples swing in place.

COUPLE FOUR

Sometimes this figure is called as follows:
```
AROUND THIS COUPLE, TAKE A LITTLE PEEP
BACK TO THE CENTRE AND SHAKE YOUR FEET
AROUND THIS COUPLE, PEEP ONCE MORE
BACK TO THE CENTRE AND COUPLE FOUR
```

COUPLE COUPLES SWING

COUPLE THROUGH COUPLE
COUPLE AROUND COUPLE
COUPLE COUPLES SWING
COUPLE FOUR

COUPLE THROUGH COUPLE
<u>COUPLE AROUND COUPLE</u>

The first couple pass between the second couple. The first gent go to the left round the second lady, while the first lady go to the right round the second gent, to places.

<u>COUPLE COUPLES SWING</u>

The first and second gents swing partners.

<u>COUPLE FOUR</u>

The first and second couples join hands four in a ring and circle left.

SHOOT THE BUFFALO

CIRCLE LEFT JUST ONCE AROUND
FIRST MAN SHOOT THE BUFFALO
CIRCLE LEFT ONCE AGAIN
SECOND MAN SHOOT -----
CIRCLE LEFT AND ON YOU GO

Circle left once round.

Without letting go hands, first man (with left elbow in front of face), followed by partner, lead through an arch made by second couple - pass behind the second man back to place - second couple unwind into hands four ring.

Repeat with second man leading.

DOUBLE BOW KNOT

or

OCEAN WAVE

CIRCLE LEFT - (FIRST COUPLE) DOUBLE BOW KNOT
CIRCLE LEFT - (SECOND COUPLE) DOUBLE BOW KNOT
CIRCLE LEFT ----

CIRCLE LEFT

The first and second couples join hands and circle once round to the left.

FIRST COUPLE - DOUBLE BOW KNOT

The first gent and second lady drop hands and the first gent lead under the arch made by the first lady and second gent. The first lady turn under her right arm and follow the first gent. The first gent then lead under an arch made by the second couple. He is followed by the first lady (still holding hands). The second gent then turn under his right arm and the two couples

CIRCLE LEFT

SECOND COUPLE - DOUBLE BOW KNOT

The second gent lead under an arch made by the second lady and first gent. The second lady turn under her right arm and follow the second gent. The second gent then lead under an arch made by the first couple. The first gent turn under his right arm and the two couples take hands four for the

CIRCLE LEFT

Note: The action for both couples in the above figure is the same.

WAVES OF THE SEA

FIRST COUPLE LEAD THROUGH AND BACK
SECOND COUPLE GO ROUND THE OUTSIDE TRACK
SECOND COUPLE LEAD THROUGH AND BACK
FIRST COUPLE GO ROUND THE OUTSIDE TRACK
HALF TURN WITH PARTNERS ALL
COUPLE UP AND CIRCLE FOUR
LEAD RIGHT ON TO THE COUPLE NEXT DOOR

First couple (crossed hands) lead in between second couple, turn in and lead back, meanwhile the second couple separate, gent left and lady right, right round the outside to each other's place.

Second couple lead forward and back, while the first couple cast, gent right and lady left, and go round the outside. Both couples half turn and join hands four in a ring and circle left.

BIG BASKET

This is a final figure for the Big Set. If the dancers happen to lose their numbers getting back in to the Grand Old Circle (big ring), it doesn't make very much difference, because they will not need their numbers any more for this part of the dance.

THE CALL:

CIRCLE LEFT
HALF-WAY AND BACK, MAKE YOUR FEET GO WHICKEDY-WHACK
GENTS TO THE CENTRE - AND BACK
LADIES TO THE CENTRE AND CIRCLE LEFT
GENTS OUTSIDE AND CIRCLE RIGHT
HALF-WAY BACK
STOP TO THE LEFT OF YOUR PARTNER, MAKE THE BASKET
CIRCLE LEFT
CORNER SWING
PARTNER SWING
PROMENADE AROUND THE RING

Description:

CIRCLE LEFT - All join hands and circle left.

HALF-WAY AND BACK - Go back to the right - still holding hands.

GENTS TO THE CENTRE AND BACK - All the gents move four steps into the ring and back out to their places.

LADIES TO THE CENTRE AND CIRCLE LEFT
GENTS OUTSIDE AND CIRCLE RIGHT - The ladies move into the centre and join hands in a circle and move to the left. The gents join hands in an outer circle round the ladies and circle to the right.

HALF-WAY BACK - Both circles reverse direction - still holding hands.

STOP TO THE LEFT OF YOUR PARTNER, MAKE THE BASKET -
The first part of the call-line is directed to the gents. They still hold hands and stop to the left of their ladies. The ladies drop hands and put their arms on the inside shoulders of the gents. The ladies are to the right of their partners.

CIRCLE LEFT - Holding the basket formation, the circle moves left.

CORNER SWING - All drop hands and corners swing.

PARTNER SWING - Partners swing once round and

PROMENADE

OPEN TUNNEL

This is another Big Set figure which can be danced when the other figures of the Big Set are finished.

The figure is started when the dancers are in the promenade position. On the call "OPEN TUNNEL" the leading couple reverse the direction and go under the arches made by all the other couples. As each couple reach the leading end, they reverse the direction and go under the arches.

When the leading couple reach the end of the "TUNNEL", they join inside hands and make an arch for the other couples to go under. When all couples have returned to the promenade position, they promenade round the hall until all the other couples have completed the arches.

THE CALL:

OPEN TUNNEL --- (with patter)
WATCH YOUR HEADS AND WATCH THEM CLOSE
IF YOU DON'T WATCH OUT WE'LL DOUBLE THE DOSE

*****

Note: If from the promenade position the leading couple make an arch first and reverse the above figure, it is called "LONDON BRIDGE".

WAGONWHEEL

```
CIRCLE LEFT
BACK TO THE RIGHT
WAGONWHEEL - GENTS TO THE CENTRE - AND BACK
LADIES TO THE CENTRE AND CIRCLE LEFT
HALF-WAY AND BACK
GENTS MOVE IN AND PICK UP YOUR PARTNERS
SWING HER OUT WITH A DOUBLE SWING
AND PROMENADE AROUND THE RING
```

CIRCLE LEFT

All join hands and circle to the left.

BACK TO THE RIGHT

All circle back to the right, still holding hands.

WAGONWHEEL - GENTS TO THE CENTRE - AND BACK

The call-line "WAGONWHEEL" lets the dancers know what to expect. The gents move four steps into the centre and back out to places.

LADIES TO THE CENTRE AND CIRCLE LEFT

The ladies move into the centre and place their right hands on the right shoulder of the lady in front of them. The circle moves to the left. The gents stand by - let the girls dance.

HALF-WAY AND BACK

The ladies reverse direction and place their left hand on the left shoulder of the lady in front.

GENTS MOVE IN AND PICK UP YOUR PARTNERS

The gents take their partner's right hand in their right hand and place their left hand on the right shoulder of their partner. The ladies stay in the circle with their left hand on the left shoulder of the lady in front. This makes the set resemble a wagonwheel.

SWING HER OUT WITH A DOUBLE SWING

Partners swing twice round and move out from the centre of the set, making a large circle for the promenade

AND PROMENADE AROUND THE RING

*****

This figure can be varied by calling it:

CIRCLE LEFT -
BACK TO THE RIGHT
LADIES TO THE CENTRE AND BACK
GENTS TO THE CENTRE AND CIRCLE LEFT
NOW ALL GO BACK THE OTHER WAY
LADIES MOVE IN AND TAKE YOUR PARTNERS
SWING OUT WITH A DOUBLE SWING
AND PROMENADE AROUND THE RING

KENTUCKY MOUNTAIN SQUARE DANCING
(RUNNING SET)

Running Set is the form of square dance which is danced in the Kentucky mountains and was seen and collected by Cecil Sharp over sixty years ago.

Most of the figures described are commonly found throughout the mountains of eastern Kentucky, and it should be remembered that they are sometimes known by different names in different parts of the State.

They are reprinted by kind permission of Pat Napier, Principal of Madison High School, Richmond, Kentucky, who was himself a Caller.

S.A. MATTHEWS